Hawk Mountain

The world's first raptor sanctuary

Text by Jim Wright
Photography by Kevin Watson

Foreword by Deborah Edge

Camino Books, Inc.
Philadelphia

1 2 3 4 5 12 11 10 09

Library of Congress Cataloging-in-Publication Data

Wright, John M.
  Hawk Mountain: the world's first raptor sanctuary / text by Jim Wright;
photography by Kevin Watson; foreword by Deborah Edge.
    p. cm.
  ISBN 978-1-933822-12-9 (alk. paper)
  1. Birds of prey—Pennsylvania—Hawk Mountain Sanctuary. 2. Birds of
prey—Pennsylvania—Hawk Mountain Sanctuary—History—Pictorial
works. 3. Hawk Mountain Sanctuary (Pa.)—History—Pictorial works. I.
Watson, Kevin. II. Title.

  QL677.78.W754 2009
  598.909748'16—dc22   2009010268

Cover and interior design: Jan Greenberg

This book is available at a special discount on bulk purchases for
promotional, business, and educational use.

Publisher
Camino Books, Inc.
P.O. Box 59026
Philadelphia, PA 19102

www.caminobooks.com

Printed in China

CREDITS:

Archival photography, the time line on page 33 and the list
of the biggest broadwing flight days were contributed by
Hawk Mountain Sanctuary Association.

The locator map on page 11 and the sanctuary map on page
57 were created by Hawk Mountain research biologist David
Barber.

The watercolor of broadwings kettling near North Lookout
on page 14 and the illustration of the northern goshawk on
page 82 are by Fred Wetzel.

The excerpt from *Hawks Aloft* by Maurice Broun and the excerpt from *The View from Hawk Mountain* by Michael Harwood are reprinted with the permission of Stackpole Books,
Mechanicsburg, Pennsylvania.

The photograph of the peregrine falcon on page 113 is courtesy of the Falcon Research Group, 2007.

The photograph of the wind turbines on page 115 is courtesy
of the *Reading Eagle*/Ben Hasty.

In memory of
Rosalie Barrow Edge,
who changed everything

"Rosalie Edge sailed almost without warning into the very center of the conservation establishment and shook it by the scruff of its neck as no one has before or since."

—Audubon historian Frank Graham Jr.,
quoted in Of a Feather, *by Scott Weidensaul*

ROSALIE BARROW EDGE (1877-1962)

North Lookout, just past sunrise

Contents

Foreword

By Deborah Edge

What is Hawk Mountain? Many images and words come immediately to mind, like family, community and permanence; nature, beauty and tranquility; innovation, education and research.

All of these speak to the core of Hawk Mountain and are beautifully represented in the pages that follow. Reading this book has brought back memories of my time spent at Hawk Mountain. I expect that it will for you as well.

I remember visiting Hawk Mountain as a child with my parents, two brothers and my grandmother, Rosalie Edge, Hawk Mountain's founder and president. My father, Peter Edge, was serving on the board of directors at the time; he and Grandmother were attending a board meeting.

For me these are hazy memories: Grandmother showing us the mountain, the North Lookout, the Common Room, meeting the eagle that lived behind Schaumboch's, and getting lost with my father and brothers on a hike to the River of Rocks.

As an adult my relationship with the mountain has become more intimate. I love to visit and watch the fall migration, hike the familiar trails, and see old friends. I am continually impressed and inspired by the work that the Hawk Mountain staff is doing both in Pennsylvania and worldwide to promote the conservation of raptors. Hawk Mountain is a unique organization and a special place to all of us who have come to know it.

I am certain that if my grandmother were alive to see Hawk Mountain today, she would be thrilled about the thousands of raptors that still fly over the North Lookout each fall, as well as the thousands of visitors who come every year to see this migration and hike the trails.

Meeting the interns who come from all over the world to learn about raptor conservation from the foremost experts in the field would be as inspirational for her as it is for me. Seeing the groups of schoolchildren learning about raptor biology would be a great excitement for her.

Hawk Mountain is a living organism that has flourished over the past 75 years while maintaining its beauty and sense of family and community.

As you peruse this book, both the photography and the text, I am sure that you, too, will find it to be a wonderful way to bring some of the mountain home with you.

MALE NORTHERN HARRIER—"GRAY GHOST"—COMING DOWN THE RIDGE

Looking east from North Lookout at sunrise

CHAPTER 1

A sense of place

"Nature offers remarkable refuge. Whatever turmoil besets the outside world, the Sanctuary remains a stronghold of peace and tranquility."

—Jim Brett, March 1974
Hawk Mountain newsletter

The weather is unseasonably warm on this October morning, and the fog in the Kempton Valley seems to take forever to lift.

With great reluctance, a visitor to Hawk Mountain's world-famous North Lookout lowers his binoculars and turns to leave.

"Some of us have to go to work," he says with a sigh.

By way of consolation, the volunteer hawk counter says that very few raptors will likely fly past the lookout on this muggy, windless day.

The words provide scant comfort. The visitor takes a final scan of the vast panorama of mountains and forests and farms arrayed before him.

Then he replies wistfully, "Sometimes, it's just being here that's important."

He's right, of course. Although the annual fall cavalcade of raptors at Hawk Mountain is a big draw, the sanctuary itself provides a deeper attraction.

As many people have come to know, this spot in rural eastern Pennsylvania is a great place to see the changing foliage. It is a great place to relax and admire the sweeping views. It is a great place to hike and to instill in children a love of nature. And it is all less than two hours from Philadelphia and New York City.

Hawk Mountain, located on the Blue Mountain, has a storied history. Every autumn from roughly the 1870s into the 1930s, this rocky land was a killing ground for thousands of migrating raptors. Weekend gunners, often from the coal mines to the north, flocked to the ridge to blast raptors out of the sky.

LOOKING TOWARD THE RIVER OF ROCKS FROM SOUTH LOOKOUT

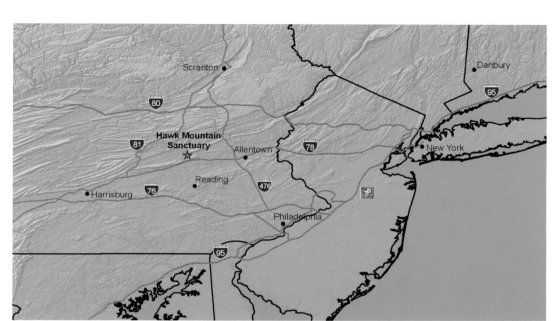

HAWK MOUNTAIN IS IN EASTERN PENNSYLVANIA NOT FAR FROM INTERSTATE 78.

Then something extraordinary happened. A New Yorker named Rosalie Barrow Edge heard about the atrocities and stepped in. In the spring of 1934, she leased a portion of the mountain where the shooting occurred—1,398 acres. That autumn, she brought in a young ornithologist, Maurice Broun, and his wife Irma to stop the massacres.

The Brouns' task appeared impossible: to persuade hard-bitten gunners, who had been shooting hawks from the ridge for as long as anybody could remember, to put aside their weapons. As Maurice Broun noted in his journal soon after his arrival, "[I] know that I'm in for one of the toughest jobs of my life."

Despite long odds, the Brouns prevailed. A place that had long been a shooting gallery became a place to protect and admire raptors. The mountain, a sacred place for the Lenape Indians centuries ago, became hallowed ground once again—a sanctuary in the truest sense.

Since those tumultuous early days, the mountain has developed a reputation as "the crossroads of naturalists." Famed birding author Roger Tory Peterson, for example, was a frequent visitor to Hawk Mountain, and he drew many of the illustrations for *Field Guide to Wildflowers* here.

RACHEL CARSON AT NORTH LOOKOUT

Biologist Rachel Carson cited declining numbers of juvenile bald eagles at Hawk Mountain in her landmark 1962 book, *Silent Spring*. Carson's book has been credited with launching the modern environmental movement. The sanctuary, through its educational and research efforts, has helped to sustain that movement.

In recent years, the sanctuary has opened the Acopian Center for Conservation Learning, a biological field station and training facility. The sanctuary has also developed a unique educational outreach program designed to boost young students' standardized test scores, introduce those children to the wonders of raptors, and help develop their love and understanding of nature.

The sanctuary is a world leader in raptor research, including the use of satellite telemetry, which enables Hawk Mountain researchers to follow the migrations of individual birds across thousands of miles.

The Acopian Center is named for its benefactor, the late Sarkis Acopian, the great conservationist and philanthropist. The center's internship program has helped spread the gospel of raptor conservation to 52 nations on six continents.

Over the past 75 years, Hawk Mountain Sanctuary has grown to 2,600 acres buffered from development by more than 12,000 acres of game lands, state forest, National Park Service land and watershed acreage.

Hawk Mountain is one link in a chain of mountains called the Appalachians, which stretch 1,500 miles from eastern Canada to

RAPTORS FASCINATE ALL AGES, INCLUDING THIS YOUNGSTER AT SOUTH LOOKOUT.

Georgia. Each fall, these mountains become a superhighway for hawks migrating to warmer climes from their northern breeding grounds.

The Kittatinny Ridge, known to the native Lenapes as the "Endless Mountain," provides a major lane on that superhighway, from eastern New York State through New Jersey and Pennsylvania to Maryland.

When there's a break in a ridge or a gap in the wind along the chain, migrating hawks gravitate southward to pick up the wind currents on the next ridge. The Kittatinny Ridge is the easternmost in the Allegheny Mountains portion of the chain, so it naturally collects raptors on their way south.

At Hawk Mountain, a huge wrinkle in the ridge creates a funnel effect. An outcropping of rocks there—North Lookout—affords consistently close views of passing hawks. And the sanctuary's experienced counters and naturalists help visitors to better appreciate what they are seeing.

"Hawk Mountain has a unique ability to help people get close to birds that are wild, and to connect with that spirit of wildness," says Laurie Goodrich, the sanctuary's senior monitoring biologist.

Thousands of birds of prey migrate past Hawk Mountain each autumn—thanks, in large part, to air currents.

Raptors rely on two types of upward air currents, thermals and deflected updraft, to migrate. Thermal air currents are rising pockets of air heated by the Sun.

Raptors use thermals to gain altitude, often in a "kettle" or flock. They then glide until they lose altitude and find another thermal to begin the process anew.

Deflected updrafts result from strong winds hitting the side of a mountain. On days with strong winds out of the north and west, raptors use these air currents to soar down the ridges.

Pictured here are broad-winged hawks kettling near North Lookout.

PAINTING BY FRED WETZEL

Hawk Mountain offers something else—an enduring sense of community. Author Michael Harwood said it best in his introduction to the millennial edition of *Hawks Aloft*: "It seems to me that—aside from the obvious role of protecting birds of prey—the most important characteristic of Hawk Mountain Sanctuary was and is the spirit of Family that has pervaded the place.... Over the years hundreds, probably thousands of sanctuary members have been so convinced of the sanctuary's message and mission that they have given it far more than their annual dues. They have come to the mountain to invest time and much energy in a piece of earth, rocks, trees, ferns, wildflowers, insects, retiles, mammals, birds and in each other."

The sanctuary's volunteers, who have helped the nonprofit sanctuary to thrive over the years, are a key part of that family.

People have met their future spouses on Hawk Mountain, formed lasting friendships, created shared memories, laughed and sometimes mourned there.

In many cases, the sanctuary has helped foster a life-long love of birds.

"It's not often you can point to a single day and say, 'This day changed my life,'" says Scott Weidensaul, a naturalist and author who grew up 30 miles away. "But one day when I was 12, my family took a trip to Hawk Mountain, and I saw an amazing number of accipiters. That day got me hooked on hawks. It got me hooked

BALD EAGLE SWOOPING THROUGH A SNOW SQUALL

on the whole concept of migration. And it was the first time I was really aware of the mountains as this unified range."

Similarly, ornithologist Peter Saenger tells of his second-grade class trip to Hawk Mountain. "That was my introduction to birds, and from that point on, I was hooked."

Saenger didn't return to Hawk Mountain until he studied ornithology in college. In the parking lot, he met a man who introduced himself as Daniel Klem, Muhlenberg College's brand-new ornithologist. Saenger transferred the next semester. Saenger now works for Professor Klem at Muhlenberg and serves as curator for the college's extensive Maurice Broun archives.

North Lookout in October

EASTERN BLUEBIRD AT NORTH LOOKOUT

Lee Schisler Jr., president of the sanctuary association, sums up the strong connection that so many people have with Hawk Mountain. "This place is in the fabric of a lot of people's being."

Hawk Mountain also offers a sense of permanence in an ever-changing world, a reassuring sense that visitors will be able to return years from now and find Hawk Mountain essentially as it is today.

The sanctuary's trails will still be mined with ankle-twisting rocks.

The lookouts should still provide breathtaking views.

The boulders at North Lookout will still provide wonderful but singularly uncomfortable seating.

The sun will still rise—often spectacularly—in the east.

And just being here at Hawk Mountain will still be what's important.

THE SIDE OF A VINTAGE BARN ON THE ROAD TO KEMPTON

Hawk Mountain is in the heart of farm country.

Carnage at Hawk Mountain: 230 dead hawks were retrieved in one day in 1932.

CHAPTER 2

The guns of Autumn

"On top of Blue Mountain above Drehersville, Schuylkill County, an appalling slaughter is going on...."

—Richard Pough, letter to Bird Lore magazine, autumn 1932

With the above words, a young conservationist named Richard Pough from Philadelphia became the first to sound an alarm.

In his letter to *Bird Lore*, Pough continued, "First [came] the broadwings in September, and out of this flight I would say 60 were shot. Then came the sharp-shinned and Cooper's hawks—thousands of these were killed.... When 100 or 150 men, armed with pump guns, automatics, and double-barreled shotguns, are sitting on top of a mountain looking for a target, no bird is safe."

The magazine forwarded the letter to the Pennsylvania authorities, suggesting they "investigate conditions on Blue Mountain with a view to better enforcement of existing laws." Not likely.

About 120 miles away, on Manhattan's Lexington Avenue, Rosalie Barrow Edge had a far more visceral reaction when she heard about the slaughter. The shooting had to stop.

As founder of the small but combative Emergency Conservation Committee, the 57-year-old Edge had already taken on the

ROSALIE EDGE AT THE SANCTUARY'S ENTRANCE

National Association of Audubon Societies because she believed it was doing too little to protect birds and wildlife. But times were tough. Banks were closing. People's finances were collapsing. The committee's income had dropped by half. Although Edge realized she could not move mountains, she was determined to save one in Pennsylvania.

In the spring of 1934, after the national Audubon group had snubbed the shooting and no other nature group would act, Edge leased roughly 1,400 acres where the most shooting occurred. The cost was $500. She also obtained an option to buy the property for $3,500—$2.50 an acre. Over the next 12 months, word of the deal and its ramifications slowly circulated. The mountain would be off-limits to hawk shooters.

It was the shot heard "round the region." As *Nature* magazine reported, "Stunned, the gun clubs and the gunners, and, it is whispered, the ammunition companies and dealers, did everything they could to block her. Lawyers were employed to try to break the lease." Nothing doing.

America was in the throes of the Great Depression, and the communities at the foot of the mountain were rough and tumble. George Hamm was a young boy back then, living near the road to the mountain. The Pennsylvania German farmer still recalls the bootleggers in a fancy convertible who secretly hired a foolhardy local farmer to mass-produce grain alcohol for them. Hamm also remembers the trucks leaving with five-gallon cans of pure, 200-proof alcohol—and the day the revenuers arrived, sidearms drawn, to shut the operation down.

In those days, says Hamm, "different guys would come to the mountain each fall to do a lot of hawk shooting—some people from here but more guys from what we used to call the Coal Region. It wasn't considered any big deal."

Enter Maurice and Irma Broun.

In the following excerpt from *Hawks Aloft*, the Brouns have just arrived at the mountain with the daunting task of keeping those gunners away from a mountain where they had hunted for decades—and a mountain they had come to consider their very own.

Broun writes in *Hawks Aloft*:

My first act in Schuylkill Haven was to phone four local newspapers, requesting each to carry a notice, for three successive days, announcing the new status of the mountain property, that it was henceforth an inviolate wildlife sanctuary, and that the trespass laws would be enforced. Then we called on Gordon Reed, the agent for the property. Oh, yes, he knew all about the mountain and all about the hawk-shoots; and he succeeded in filling us with gloom. I told him that I was about to put up no-trespassing posters along the road, especially at the beginning of the trail that led through the woods to the shooting stands. When we parted, Mr. Reed suggested, "After you get your posters up, take my advice and scram!"

Early morning found me putting up posters along the rocky road. Where did the bounds of the property run through the woods? Not even the neighboring owners could tell exactly. Five years later a costly survey revealed to us the extent of the 1398 acres. For the time being, it was necessary to post both sides of a stretch of road one and a half miles; for the road, a public thoroughfare, bisected the Sanctuary. It was dreadfully hot. I was surprised that no hunters had come. I did not know that it was too early in the season, nor did I realize that the hawk-hunters knew just when to flock to the mountain.

MAURICE BROUN, HAWK MOUNTAIN'S FIRST CURATOR

By mid-afternoon the lonely road flaunted posters every few yards. A local game warden, apparently startled by my newspaper notices which had just been printed, came to find out what it was all about. The warden tried to impress me with the utter futility of my job. "Wait till the coal-miners from Tamaqua come along; then you'll see," he warned me. While we argued, two carloads of hunters drove up—the vanguard. I explained that hunting of all kinds was henceforth prohibited. There was much guttural, explosive language from the visitors. But they left the mountain, bewildered, to say the least. In the days to follow I was to meet many such men, many of whom I tried to reason with as to why hawks should not be killed indiscriminately. Generally, these men were irritated, unwilling to listen. The game warden, a man named Jones, concluded his visit with the statement that I had the hardest job on my hands that I'd ever have in my life. "You can't stop those guys from shooting hawks up here," he said, notwithstanding that I had already done so, before his eyes!

It suddenly came to me that, after all, in spite of our right, our duty to stop the hawk-shooting, we were, from the standpoint of the hunters, meddlesome outsiders, and as such we were bound to arouse indignation. Of course, it did not matter to the hunters that most of the hawks also came down

IRMA BROUN, "THE KEEPER OF THE GATE"

GUNNERS HUNG THIS RED-TAILED HAWK FROM THE BRIDGE IN DREHERSVILLE AS A WARNING TO THE BROUNS.

from New England and New York. Did they ever give a thought to the rights of others?

Before the close of the day I prepared a thousand-word statement—"A New Deal for Hawks"—defending the action of the Emergency Conservation Committee in leasing the mountaintop to prevent the killing of hawks. It hammered out the theme of unjust persecution and the economic importance of the hawks. Every trip up and down the mountain was agony and torture to tires, but I sent the article off the same evening to three local newspapers, whose combined circulation exceeded 200,000. The article promptly appeared in print, and it was copied in other newspapers, as far away as Scranton.

Daybreak of our third day on the mountain found me patrolling the road! I was anxious to see some hawks, but I was utterly ignorant of the hawk-flights and their modus operandi. And, naively, I expected to see hunters at that ridiculous hour. During the night someone had ripped off most of the no-trespassing posters.

At breakfast, a few staccato shots echoed from the pinnacle that Mrs. Merkle had pointed out to us. I dashed up the road and through the woods, over an exceedingly rough but well-trodden path to the pinnacle. There I found a young man and his father, from Allentown, settled behind a huge rock slab. Their presence was pardonable, since the posters had been abstracted. And were they surprised to learn that the area was now a sanctuary!

A VINTAGE SANCTUARY LOGO

Had they killed any hawks? Not yet—the birds had just begun to come. They departed like gentlemen after—of all things—a brief discussion of the geology of the region, about which I confessed that I knew less than they. Then for the first time I saw the great rock promontory, and the scene that suddenly spread out before me was one of great beauty.

As I patrolled the road that day, replacing posters, I was impressed with the countless numbers of old cartridge shells scattered along a quarter-mile stretch of road above the present entrance to the Sanctuary. In the early afternoon I was thrilled to see my first flight of hawks, some fifty birds, including three bald eagles, three peregrine falcons, a few broadwings and sharpshins, all passing fairly low over the road. This was exciting!

During the day three more cars came up, with seven inquiring faces, and shotguns ready for business. But they departed promptly. One of the men made a slurring remark about the "New York chiselers going to hog all the shooting."

I had had abundant experience with trespassers and game-law violators, at various wildlife refuges in New England. But this situation was far more complex; it involved the interests of hundreds, possibly thousands, of organized, politically-ruled men who were certain to boil up in anger and resentment at the intrusion of a small, to them unheard-of, organization which had suddenly seized "their" entire mountain. Though we possessed maps and land titles, the location of the twelve miles of boundaries of the wilderness property was anybody's guess. Were we sitting on a powder keg? To withdraw was unthinkable.

A turning point came on Sunday, October 7, 1934. Although earlier weekends had been rainy, this Sunday was crisp and clear, ideal for hawks, and the Brouns feared that mobs of hunters might converge on the mountain.

Sure enough, standing on what is now North Lookout in early afternoon, Maurice Broun heard shotgun fire about a half-mile away. He and two friends hastened to that area, only to find ten armed men standing just beyond the sanctuary's property line.

A standoff of several minutes ensued, until, as Broun recounted in *Hawks Aloft*, one of the armed men lowered his gun and approached him, threatening: "I'll knock your block off."

But Broun stood his ground, and the man finally backed away, muttering: "You damn hawk-lovers; you're just a bunch of barbarians."

When Broun and his two companions returned to the lookout, they found that a mob had indeed arrived. "That day seventy-four men, women and children climbed to the Lookout to enjoy the beautiful scenery and the birds," Broun wrote.

That same day, a security guard at the entrance had turned away 32 hunters. In years past, there would have been five or ten times that number.

The tide had turned. That day, twice as many people had come to the mountain to see hawks as to kill them.

As Broun noted in *Hawks Aloft*, in the autumn of 1934, he and Irma "had the satisfaction of seeing more than ten thousand hawks pass safely; not a single bird was killed."

The sanctuary—the first of its kind in the world—was a success. That first year, Hawk Mountain drew 500 visitors.

In 1935, with five-foot-tall, 100-pound Irma Broun standing guard to turn away hunters and greet birders, the sanctuary tallied 1,250 visitors. She soon became known as "keeper of the gate," the first volunteer for Hawk Mountain.

A year later, more than 3,300 people traveled the steep dirt road. As Maurice Broun noted in an Emergency Conservation Committee report, "Cameras and field glasses have [supplanted] the shotguns of the old days."

In 1937, Pennsylvania passed a law protecting all hawks but sharp-shinned hawks, Cooper's hawks and northern goshawks.

In 1938, the Emergency Conservation Committee secured clear title to the land and deeded it to the newly minted Hawk Mountain Sanctuary Association. Rosalie Edge became the sanctuary's first president, and Maurice Broun its curator.

Yet the story of the Hawk Mountain Sanctuary and the slaughter of raptors were far from over. Putting 1,400 acres off-limits to gunners protected hawks only while they migrated past one small section of the Kittatinny Ridge. The ridges of eastern Pennsylvania provided plenty of other places where gunners could still shoot raptors.

Edge and Broun campaigned tirelessly for all raptors, trying to prove to the public and the lawmakers that protected hawks were being killed.

THIS IS ONE OF THE CLICKERS THAT MAURICE BROUN USED TO COUNT HAWKS.

In 1949 came the publication of *Hawks Aloft*. Broun had begun it one winter while snowed in on the mountain. For writing paper, he used the backs of Christmas cards he and Irma had received.

Change came slowly. Electricity didn't come to the mountain until 1951. Hunters remained unenlightened. In local newspapers, outdoors columnists continued to rail against raptors. They complained that the hawks were killing racing pigeons and other birds, and that "the only good hawk is a dead one."

One columnist for the *Pottsville Journal* wrote of a family of hawks that lived in the woods near a pen of racing pigeons. "We do not know [the hawks'] species or if they are protected," he wrote. "All we do know is that there is a shotgun and rifle with shells handy standing at a convenient place near the pen. When one of these hawks comes within gun range, it is going to be made into a good hawk regardless of any ornithological societies, game protectors, or what have you. The species of those hawks will be determined after the gun cracks and the hawk lies dead on the ground."

Hunters also continued to kill raptors from outcroppings on other parts of the Kittatinny Ridge.

According to Fred Wetzel, who as a youth spent his weekends with the Brouns and who later became assistant curator of the sanctuary, Broun tried to persuade visitors to visit other ridges. He believed that if birdwatchers showed up in numbers, the shooters would back off.

"But Maurice was having an awful time," says Wetzel. "People refused to get involved because it was too dangerous. If you went up there on a lookout as an adult with binoculars, you'd frequently have shot flying over your head. These guys did not like birdwatchers or anybody who was up there."

In 1952, when Wetzel turned 16 and became old enough to drive, Broun had him and four other young men go undercover to prove that gunners would shoot anything with talons and feathers. Wetzel went to Bake Oven Knob, a lookout so popular for hunters that it had 11 blinds for various wind conditions. Two other groups went to the blinds along the ridge at Little Gap and at Route 183. Wetzel claimed that he was a taxidermy student—which he was—and that he wanted to collect the dead birds so he could use them for practice.

To prove the massacre was still continuing, Broun had Wetzel and the other young men bring the carcasses to Hawk Mountain and pile them by the entrance.

"I remember one time we came up with 847 dead raptors in our cars, and that's a big pile of birds," Wetzel says. "It included one osprey, two peregrines, an immature bald eagle and all sorts of other hawks. Maurice used to estimate that on a good flight day, less than half the birds migrating along the ridge actually got through that section of Pennsylvania."

With that kind of graphic evidence, Edge and Broun eventually got the law changed. In 1956, they won protection for all hawks in northeastern Pennsylvania during the months of September and October. Not until 1970, after Broun had retired, did laws give diurnal raptors year-round protection throughout the state.

Even so, Wetzel says, illegal shooting continued, for the simple reason that hunters seldom got caught. The sanctuary's second curator, Alex Nagy, and Hawk Mountain staff tried to change that as well. They would go to the hunting blinds, hide in the woods, then report the license plates of shooters who killed hawks and drove off with them.

MAURICE BROUN AND ROGER TORY PETERSON

Today, reports of hawk shooting are rare, and public attitudes have changed.

In the mid-'60s, naturalist Roger Tory Peterson put the sanctuary's leadership in raptor protection into proper perspective.

"Certainly Hawk Mountain, more than any other spot in our country, has dramatized the birds of prey. It has caught the public imagination and has done more to help people think rationally about the place in nature of these much maligned birds. Today it is only the biologically illiterate sportsman who shoots hawks."

These conservationists retrieved dozens of hawks at Bake Oven Knob in the 1950s.

Hawk Mountain Sanctuary chronology

1932 Richard Pough goes to Blue Mountain on a September Sunday and witnesses the hawk slaughter, reporting it in *Bird Lore*, precursor to *Audubon* magazine.

1933 Pough speaks about the hawk carnage to a New York City meeting of conservationists. In the audience is Rosalie Edge, head of the Emergency Conservation Committee.

1934 In the spring, Edge visits the mountain and later obtains a lease on 1,400 acres for $500. In September, she hires Maurice Broun to stop the shooting. Later that fall, Broun begins to monitor and count the migrating birds.

1937 A Pennsylvania law protects all hawks except the goshawk, Cooper's and sharp-shinned.

1938 The Emergency Conservation Committee secures clear title to Hawk Mountain and deeds it to the newly incorporated Hawk Mountain Sanctuary Association; Rosalie Edge is its first president.

1943-45 No counts of migrating raptors are recorded during World War II.

1946 The sanctuary begins year-round operations.

1962 As evidence of pesticides' impact, Rachel Carson cites the decline of juvenile bald eagles seen in migration counts at Hawk Mountain in *Silent Spring*.

1967 South Lookout is opened.

1972 Widespread use of DDT is banned in the United States.

1974 The Visitor Center opens.

1976 Hawk Mountain begins its college-level internship program, with Seth Benz as the first participant.

1986 Hawk Mountain welcomes its first international intern, Manachem Adar, a student from Israel.

1988 To the great relief of visitors to North Lookout, an outhouse is built nearby after the construction materials and composting toilet are brought in by helicopter.

1991 The expanded Joseph and Helen Taylor Visitor Center opens.

2001 Hawk Mountain Sanctuary acquires 43 acres and breaks ground for its Acopian Center for Conservation Learning. The center opens in Autumn 2002.

2006 The 70th Annual Hawkwatch records more than 25,000 raptors, including record numbers of golden eagles and merlins, and record-tying numbers of peregrine falcons.

2009 The sanctuary marks its 75th anniversary.

The seating at North Lookout may be Spartan, but the view is unsurpassed.

CHAPTER 3

> "And these whitened limestone rocks on which I am sitting—these, too, were formed under that Paleozoic ocean, of the myriad tiny skeletons of creatures that drifted in its water. Now I lie back with half-closed eyes and try to realize that I am at the bottom of another ocean—an ocean of air on which the hawks are sailing."
>
> — Rachel Carson,
> **Road of the Hawks**

North Lookout

By any yardstick, the trip to North Lookout (1521 feet above sea level) is an experience.

The one-mile hike from the trail entrance is partly uphill, with a 300-foot rise in elevation. About halfway, the trail becomes increasingly rocky and occasionally slippery. And you lug your own food and water because what you brought is what you'll have.

For many first-timers, there's a sense of achievement in just getting to the lookout. If getting there were easy, it wouldn't be quite the same.

Once you reach North Lookout, there's no place to sit but a massive pile of rocks. Think of it as nature's amphitheater for masochists.

The winds here can be brisk. If you're visiting in late fall and winter, they can be downright bone-numbing. Some regulars talk about going to the lookout in January in sub-freezing temperatures, bundled up, drinking soup and coffee and—in an effort to keep the blood circulating in their feet—walking around in a circle tromped in the snow.

SCENES FROM
THE CROWD

A BALD EAGLE FLIES PAST NORTH LOOKOUT.

RED-BACKED VOLES LOVE
NORTH LOOKOUT IN THE FALL,
WHEN PLENTY OF PEOPLE ARE
AROUND TO FEED THEM.

Even when the temperature is above 40 degrees and your socks are wool, keeping your feet warm can be a challenge.

As one of Hawk Mountain's longtime regulars, Bob Lynn, puts it: "Up on North, you can have sun, hail, rain, sleet, snow—all on the same day."

All of this raises a question. Why do so many people think this lookout is the closest place to heaven?

First, there's the view. If the view from the more-easily reached South Lookout is singular, then the view from North Lookout is, well, doubly so. From South Lookout, you can see the Kempton Valley and beyond, clear to Bethlehem. From North Lookout, you can see all of that, plus the entire other side of the Kittatinny Ridge, including the Poconos (see panorama, pages 52-53).

A CHIPMUNK ENJOYS A CHESTNUT—
CHESTNUT TREES WERE ONCE
PLENTIFUL AT NORTH LOOKOUT.

The birding is likely to be better, too, and not just for sharp-shinned hawks and redtails. In early autumn, on the edges of the outcropping, you are apt to see cedar waxwings, bluebirds, and migrating warblers ranging from Cape Mays to blackpolls.

The more people are on the rocks, the more pairs of eyes on the sky and the greater the amount of chatter. Regulars reminisce, catch up on news, talk about recent bird sightings, and ooh-and-ah when an occasional sharp-shinned hawk attacks the owl decoy that watches over the lookout.

Part of the experience is the sense of community there. In Maurice Broun's *Hawks Aloft*, a naturalist referred to the sanctuary as a "school in the clouds," and that is particularly true at North Lookout. Broun described this school as a place "where one sees and learns about nature in an effortless manner, where knowledge of nature is tempered with humor, kindled with good fellowship, sparked by the inspiration of many inquiring minds and kindred spirits, whose common ideal is the simple creed: 'Live and let live.'"

It is a place where children and retirees, professors and bus drivers, birders and beginners rub elbows, all created equal under their binoculars.

For Mary Bailey, who has lived in nearby Eckville all her life and who went birding with Broun in the 1930s and 1940s, Hawk Mountain in general and North Lookout in particular changed her outlook on life.

"I felt uneasy around people with an education. But you'd come up here, you'd talk to people, and you'd find out they're doctors, nurses, lawyers," she says. "You have conversations and learn that you know as much as they do about a lot of things…. I learned you need people from all walks of life."

Although hawk-watching is more intense with many eyes scanning the skies, being alone at North Lookout also has its appeal.

The early hours are a favorite part of the day because everything is quiet. When the lookout gets packed with spectators, fewer non-raptors perch nearby. With fewer human distractions, you become far more aware of the world around you. The sky seems bigger. The view seems endless. The universe seems vaster.

The word often used to describe the experience—especially at dawn or dusk—is "spiritual."

A year or two ago, on August 15, the first day of the official raptor-counting season, longtime Hawk Mountaineer Eugene Rohrbach arrived at North Lookout just as the sun began to rise over a foggy Kempton Valley. For Rohrbach, this was the best time of day to be there. "It's so quiet," he says. "I can be alone and talk to God."

Charlie Gant, or "Broadwing Charlie," has returned to Hawk Mountain almost every September for some 70 years, and he still tells of a late afternoon one November when he and then-Curator Jim Brett had North Lookout to themselves.

"It was rather blustery, and finally everybody left by about a quarter to five," says Gant. "But the sun broke through just before it set. Right about then, on a fairly good wind, two golden eagles came by, with the sun catching the glint on their feathers.

"Jim said, 'That makes it a red-letter day.'"

Hawk-watching can be helped by a few clouds—the raptors are easier to spot against a white background.

SETTING UP FOR THE DAY'S COUNT

How the raptors get counted

The front line for the count is "the pit," that nest of rocks at North Lookout. Every day, from mid-August to mid-December, from dawn to dusk, wildlife biologists and trained volunteers keep track of the numbers of falcons, hawks, vultures, and eagles that zoom down the Kittatinny Ridge on their way south.

Although the view from this pile of Tuscarora sandstone on a clear autumn day can take one's breath away, little is glamorous about hawk counting. It requires eagle eyes, constant attention, an acute knowledge of raptor identification, a disregard for creature comforts and—especially in December—a very warm wardrobe.

The counter's day typically begins before sun-up when he or she arrives at the mountain and treks the rocky three-fourths of a mile from Hawk Mountain Road up to North Lookout. As soon as the counter arrives at the pit, he or she readies the few tools of the trade and starts the day's count.

The counter's tools are mostly low-tech—three counting mechanisms that have changed little in decades. Two are manual clickers to count the most frequent fliers for that time of autumn. A multiple clicker called a Denominator has six buttons to record age and sex data or to count non-raptors.

Every hour, on a "scratch" sheet, the counter tabulates the totals for ospreys, northern harriers, three species of accipiter, three

A DENOMINATOR IS USED TO KEEP TRACK OF AGE AND SEX DATA AND TO COUNT NON-RAPTORS.

species of buteos, three species of falcons, two species of vultures and two species of eagles. At ten minutes after the hour, he or she uses a walkie-talkie to report the data to the Visitor Center. The information is then posted at several spots in the sanctuary so visitors have a sense of the day's migration.

Typically, at least one volunteer is on hand from the outset to scan the skies for birds. As the sun climbs in the sky, more and more birders arrive. By noon the outcropping can be jammed with birders, hikers and tourists out to see the daily air show.

On most days, two counters conduct the count—one does the raw numbers and one attempts to record the age and the sex of

MANUAL CLICKERS ARE USED TO COUNT FREQUENT FLIERS.

the birds, as well as record other migrants such as songbirds, waterfowl, dragonflies, and monarch butterflies. One can calculate the age of a sharp-shinned or Cooper's hawk by the color of its plumage, and Hawk Mountain is one of the few raptor-census sites where the birds fly so close that counters can sometimes see that kind of detail.

To the casual observer, the job may appear glamorous, but it's hard to maintain a steady focus for hours on end, let alone be able to distinguish one raptor species from another as the birds whiz past—sometimes dozens at a time. On big-number days, the counters divide the view in half, with each scanning a part of the sky.

"I look at a specific area of the sky and count the birds as they go by," says Hawk Mountain research biologist David Barber. "When the birds just keep streaming past, it's exhilarating and exhausting. But when the day's over, you're just tired and hungry—you probably haven't even had time to eat."

At day's end, the counter treks down the mountain to the Visitor Center to post the day's count on the Hawk Mountain Web site and update the automated phone recording (610-756-6000, extension 7). The Hawk Mountain site, hawkmountain.org, also includes the updated yearly totals and posts the results automatically to an e-mail list. Some 3,000 people subscribe to the list, and during the migration months, the sanctuary's Web site gets between 2,000 and 6,000 hits a day.

The whole process at day's end takes from ten to forty minutes, depending on how hectic that day has been. The results are typically posted within an hour after sundown for birders around the globe to see.

THE GREAT HORNED OWL DECOY ATTRACTS AN OCCASIONAL RAPTOR, TO THE DELIGHT OF ONLOOKERS.

Raptor counters at North Lookout

"A Good Day at Hawk Mountain"

In his much-admired 1973 book, *The View from Hawk Mountain*, Michael Harwood captures the anticipation and excitement on North Lookout on a memorable day. Here are excerpts from the first chapter:

The first hawk of the day appears, soundlessly, rising out of the trees below us this fine, mid-September morning. The time is not yet nine o'clock daylight-saving time—eight o'clock bird time as we say, or standard time. The day is warm, the fog is burning out of the valleys, and obviously the air has begun to rise a little, stirring the hawk's impulse to get moving south. It flaps once or twice, then stretches its rounded wings flat into a plane about three feet from tip to tip, and turns slowly in a small circle, feeling for the buoyant air that will lift it. The bird's back and wings are brown, with a touch of olive; the short tail is barred with wide black and white stripes.

"There's a broadwing," says one of my companions on North Lookout. This is a weekday, but already there are six of us sitting here on favored boulders, facing east along the spine of the Kittatinny Ridge.

"He isn't getting much lift yet."

As it circles below us, the broad-winged hawk manages the air with slight adjustments of its tail and wing feathers. It spreads the tail and the primaries—the first 10 feathers at the back edge of each wing, from the wing tip in; spreads them wide to catch the air, closes a few, twists them for control as it turns, draws all together as it sideslips, spreads the feathers again, circles, flaps once, twice, three times for more altitude, circles—not yet at eye level, feathers twisting, flaring, narrowing, flicking. It is unbelievable that any creature should have such delicate control over so many of its parts. To describe what man does in his winged machines as "flying" is more than generous; compared to the hawk, man just bangs the air, slams through it.

"Well, buddy, where are your brethren?"—addressed to the hawk.

"It's early yet."

"Oh-oh, there they are: one, two, three, four—see, Charlie, under the Hunters' Field."

"Right. I've got another bunch over here, to the left of that."

BLACK-THROATED GREEN WARBLER AT NORTH LOOKOUT

BLACK-THROATED BLUE WARBLER AT NORTH LOOKOUT

Someone else finds a third group, then a fourth. Broadwings that set down on the ridge at the end of yesterday's flight are now getting up from perches all over the slopes below us, circling for altitude, seeking the updrafts, ganging up into the groups in which they will travel. This looks to be a good day at Hawk Mountain.

The Kittatinny Ridge rises in New York State and, virtually unbroken, marches across northern New Jersey and eastern Pennsylvania all the way to the Maryland border. The Indians gave the ridge its name; Kittatinny means "endless mountain." There are some short outrider ridges between this ridge and the distant sea, but the Kittatinny is essentially the southeast edge of the Appalachian chain.

When the hawks leave their breeding territories in eastern Canada and the northeastern states and move toward the south in the fall—some to winter in New England, some to stop in the Middle Atlantic states, some to go on, even as far as South America—many of them make for the Atlantic coastline and follow that. But large numbers, particularly of the hawks that like to soar, stay inland and follow the Appalachians. The heat rising and the wind rebounding off the mountains provides lift—sheets of rising air, row upon row of combers in the sky—on which they can ride and so cover long distances with relatively little effort.

The Kittatinny is the last of the great ridges they reach. When the hawks reach the endless mountain, a good many of them stay with it. On some days they pile up along the ridge by the thousands.

Most migration seems to take place almost by magic. You don't see it happening, partly because so much of it goes on at night; suddenly one morning the city park or the front lawn is swarming with robins or towhees or white-throated sparrows. But at Hawk Mountain the flow of southing birds is visible; it goes on and on during a good day, giving an inkling of the breadth and depth of the movement.

Wherever I am, when the wind is in the northwest and the air has a bite to it, the view from Hawk Mountain spreads itself before me in my memory and I long to be a part of it— the ancient upthrust mountains, the enormous space, the rhythms of weather, the passing of birds that are the essence of wildness, all speaking of measures of time that dwarf man.

A JUVENILE CEDAR WAXWING EATS AN AMERICAN MOUNTAIN ASH BERRY.

By eleven o'clock, North and South Lookouts have counted between them more than 900 broadwings, plus a scattering of other hawks. Not bad, but this evidently isn't The Day after all. We should have seen a couple of thousand broadwings by now.

The wind dies. In the four hours between eleven and three, not a single hawk passes either North or South Lookout. Now people have begun to stir from their rocks, pack up their gear, and head down the mountain; this late, after such an empty spell, not much is likely to happen.

NORTH LOOKOUT, THEN KNOWN SIMPLY AS "THE LOOKOUT," IN THE 1950s

A few minutes after four, one of the watchers, scanning the sky, aims his binoculars over the broad valley to the north and shouts in astonishment. There is a huge boil of birds out there; already some of the hawks have set, are past us, and are streaking toward the west. The count taker sits up, snatches his binoculars to his eyes with one hand, takes his mechanical counter in the other and starts pressing the plunger rapidly, registering some 300 broadwings the next five minutes.

As the last of them glide past, I track back along the path they followed until I am looking at the ridge. Even at two miles, I can see there are hundreds and hundreds of birds there—a storm of broadwings.

For several minutes there is no end to them. I find myself standing with my arms spread wide toward the birds.

And then they are gone. In less than 15 minutes, we have seen more than a thousand broadwings.

The view to the left of North Lookout includes the train tracks and the Little Schuylkill River

McKEANSBURG NEW RINGGOLD NORTH PINNACLE LEFT HUNTERS' FIELD HUNTERS' FIELD

This panoramic view from North Lookout includes all the major hawk-watching landmarks.

5　4　3　2　1　DONAT　RIVER OF ROCKS　PINNACLE　OWL'S HEAD　HEMLOCK HEIGHTS

A VIEW OF THE PATH LOOKING TOWARD THE TRAILHEAD AND HAWK MOUNTAIN ROAD

The places you'll see

CHAPTER 4

"How you manage to get yourself to Hawk Mountain on a workday is your problem....

"Me? I called in sick—from the payphone at the convenience store just after you turn off 61 North. 'A cold [front],' I explained to my boss, sniffing grandly for effect. 'Woke up this morning [to northwest winds] and just felt miserable [at the thought of missing a good hawk flight]. Absolutely miserable.'

"By the time I reached the parking area, I found my condition much improved. By the time I reached the gate guarding the entrance to the trail, I felt splendid. Nothing like a trip to Hawk Mountain to make all things right with the world again."

— Pete Dunne, Feather Quest

Hawk Mountain is about a lot more than migrating raptors. The sanctuary offers many areas worth a visit almost any time of year. Here's a quick tour, with a look at a sanctuary tradition or two along the way.

The Visitor Center, adjacent to the parking areas, is the best place to start at Hawk Mountain. The center offers education displays and programs that often feature live raptors, as well as a Wings of Wonder raptor gallery featuring life-size carvings of the raptors that typically pass Hawk Mountain. You can also get free maps and all sorts of information about the sanctuary and raptor-watching. A well-stocked bookstore and a wide selection of binoculars and bird-oriented gifts are also among the attractions.

LIVE RAPTOR DEMONSTRATION IN THE VISITOR CENTER

By the parking lots and just beyond the Visitor Center is an amphitheater where, weather permitting, several of the live-raptor shows are presented on weekends in the spring and fall.

On the path to Hawk Mountain Road and the trail entrance is the **Native Plant Garden**, one of the sanctuary's many treasures. Once a gravel parking lot, the site was converted into a habitat landscaped with more than 100 native perennials that bloom from late March to October. An array of native flowering plants attracts a kaleidoscope of butterflies during the warmer months.

The garden features a bird-observation blind, a small waterfall and a pond abounding in cattails, lily pads, frogs and dragonflies.

The garden is also home to a huge steel-rod sculpture of a golden eagle, "Spirit of the Heart" by the noted nature artist Mary Taylor. Her osprey sculpture can be found inside the Visitor Center.

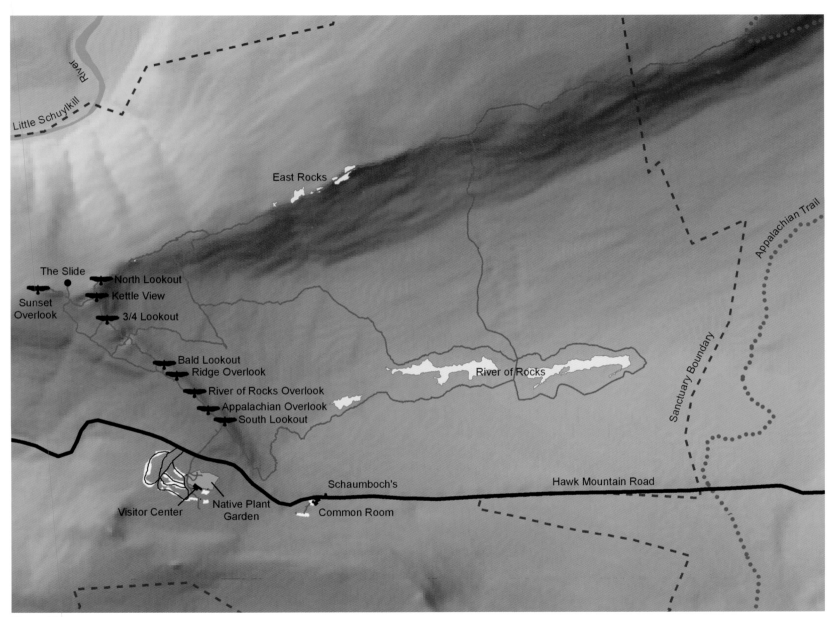

River

Little Schuylkill

East Rocks

The Slide

North Lookout

Kettle View

Sunset
Overlook

3/4 Lookout

Bald Lookout

Ridge Overlook

River of Rocks Overlook

Appalachian Overlook

South Lookout

River of Rocks

Sanctuary Boundary

Appalachian Trail

Visitor Center

Native Plant
Garden

Schaumboch's

Common Room

Hawk Mountain Road

HAWK MOUNTAIN SITES AND TRAILS

TIGER LILIES IN THE NATIVE PLANT GARDEN

GREAT SPANGLED FRITILLARY ON WILD BERGAMOT IN THE
NATIVE PLANT GARDEN

South Lookout (1,300 feet above sea level) is only 300 yards from the Visitor Center, across Hawk Mountain Road, and the terrain is far less challenging than the trek to North Lookout.

The lookout has a beautiful view of the Kempton Valley and Kittatinny Ridge. A few oak benches provide places to sit. And it is accessible by most motorized wheelchairs.

On days when the raptors are cutting across the valley instead of along the ridge, South Lookout can offer a great vantage point.

South Lookout was added in 1968. Before then, North Lookout was simply called the Lookout, and the trail ran diagonally instead of making a left turn at South Lookout.

One of the first things you notice as you gaze out on the Kempton Valley from South Lookout is the River of Rocks. The "River," light-gray gashes in the woodlands at the base of the mountain, is a boulder field formed during the last Ice Age, when the constant

SOUTH LOOKOUT

HALFWAY ROCK

freezing and melting slowly moved the sandstone boulders down the mountainside.

And yes, you can actually hear the spring gurgling under the rocks after the spring snowmelt. That's why Maurice Broun dubbed it "the upside-down river."

The River of Rocks is part of a depression called **The Kettle**. The river eventually flows aboveground, when it becomes Kettle Creek.

If you've been to Hawk Mountain a few times, you've probably noticed staffers and a few regulars carrying beautiful leather-reinforced **pack baskets**. The tradition had its start with Maurice Broun, who on occasion would carry gear in a trapper's basket. Jim Brett also popularized it when he was curator.

Brett had used a large pack basket ever since he made one from a kit as a Boy Scout. When he got to Hawk Mountain, he quickly discovered that the baskets, made from woven oak strips, could not withstand the rocky terrain. His solution was to protect the top and the bottom of the basket with leather.

The baskets proved so practical and durable that a Hawk Mountain staffer, Phil Haas, began to make them in the early 1980s. In 1984, he made some highly popular, smaller baskets, which he numbered. Mark Hamm has made the baskets in recent years and sells them out of his wife's shop in Kutztown, Collene's Crafts and Flowers.

The baskets' appeal goes far beyond aesthetics. "I like that we can carry clipboard and lunch, and nothing is crushed," says the sanctuary's senior monitoring biologist Laurie Goodrich. "I also like that it can be used as a table in the field."

Most people seem to be in a hurry to get to North Lookout in autumn, and the **North Lookout Trail** is often considered a trudge.

If you're not in a rush, the trail offers several other lookouts (including the aforementioned South), a small but notable rock, and all sorts of sights and side paths along the way.

An aerial view of the River of Rocks and The Kettle. Can you find North Lookout?

THE RIVER OF ROCKS

The notable rock is **Halfway Rock**, or so some Hawk Mountain regulars have dubbed it. It is near the halfway point between the road and North Lookout, and its strange shape and location (right in the middle of the trail) make it one of the few memorable rocks on the way.

If you scan the ground carefully along the path to North Lookout, you can see everything from toads to chipmunks, as well as an assortment of fungi.

About two thirds of the way, you have a choice of routes—the Express Trail, which involves a steeper climb, and the longer scenic route, which includes stairs with handrails and a bit of history.

At the bottom of the stairs to North Lookout is a beautiful glen called the **Hall of the Mountain King**, named by Irma Broun after one of the movements in Edvard Grieg's *Peer Gynt Suite*.

This part of the mountain was the site of industrial activity in the 1800s, when sand was excavated there to make glass.

At first, mules transported the sand down the trail to the road. Later, a stone company built a narrow-gauge gravity railway down the mountain's steep northwest slope to the Little Schuylkill River and a nearby railroad track. The sand was loaded into railcars at the Hall of the Mountain King, transported through a cut in the mountain, and then sent down **The Slide**, as that steep slope was called.

THE SCENIC ROUTE, THROUGH THE HALL OF THE MOUNTAIN KING

AMERICAN TOAD NEAR THE TRAIL

The mountainside in those days had been cleared, with the felled trees used to make charcoal. As a result, the top of The Slide became a favorite spot for gunners. Richard Pough took his historic photographs of slaughtered hawks there in the early 1930s. These days the view is overgrown, but people still report finding an occasional shotgun shell—more than 75 years later.

The sanctuary also offers more than **eight miles of trails**, including the 4-mile River of Rocks Trail, the 1.7-mile Golden Eagle Trail, and the 2.5-mile Skyline Trail.

All of them have more than their fair share of rocks. Allow plenty of time, bring a trail map, wear boots or sturdy shoes, carry plenty of water, and pack a cell phone (for emergency use). The trails have blazes—and numbered markers when they cross one another so you can report your location if you get lost.

As you approach the sanctuary from the west on Route 895, you can see the sanctuary's **Acopian Center for Conservation Learning**, Hawk Mountain's research and training facility, where the ornithologists, monitoring biologists and interns work and study.

Just after you turn right onto Hawk Mountain Road, you'll cross a modern bridge over the Little Schuylkill River. In 1934, on an earlier bridge at this location, a gunner hung a dead red-tailed hawk in an effort to intimidate Maurice and Irma Broun.

As you approach the sanctuary from the east on Hawk Mountain Road, you may notice a turnoff for **Pine Swamp Road** and then—about a mile later—another turnoff as you enter Eckville. The road is a loop, and if you make the second left and go a half-mile or so, you'll find some good warbler spots in the spring and fall. The area can also provide some good owling.

At the foot of Hawk Mountain, the 2,174-mile **Appalachian Trail** crosses Hawk Mountain Road, and you can park on the side of the road if you'd like to walk along the trail. Cross the road and you'll go eight-tenths of a mile to the State Game Lands. Continue on the trail and you're headed toward Georgia. To the right, you can hike across Kettle Creek. If you continue on the Appalachian Trail, you'll eventually reach Maine.

After you enter the sanctuary property, you'll see a large brown building called **the Common Room** on your left, where seminars are held and school groups gather.

Just before the Common Room, you'll note a white house at the roadside on your right. This place is known as **Schaumboch's**,

THE NEARBY APPALACHIAN TRAIL PROVIDES ADDITIONAL HIKING OPPORTUNITIES.

and its history would fill a book unto itself. The condensed version is that the house was built in the late 1700s and soon became a rest stop for anyone traveling the road over the mountain.

The place gained notoriety in the 1850s when a tavern keeper named Matthias Schambacher took over. Soon after, travelers started to disappear. The place would soon be called Schaumboch's, and the rumor was that the innkeeper would ply overnight guests with local applejack and then take them to the barn and kill them with an ax.

Schaumboch's

The hotel operated into the 1920s, when Prohibition put it out of business, and moonshiners took over. Maurice and Irma Broun moved into the cottage in 1938, after the sanctuary association purchased the building and its three acres of orchards. Although the Brouns attributed the strange noises they heard at night to wood rats, Hawk Mountain staffers have reported some ghostly activities over the years.

In the late 1970s, psychic Alex Tanous and parapsychologist Karlis Osis held a séance in Schaumboch's. Their findings seemed to confirm the local legends—and those unexplainable occurrences seen and heard by Hawk Mountain staff.

Schaumboch's is not open to the public. It is the private residence of the sanctuary's director of facilities, who insists the ghostly presences have made themselves scarce.

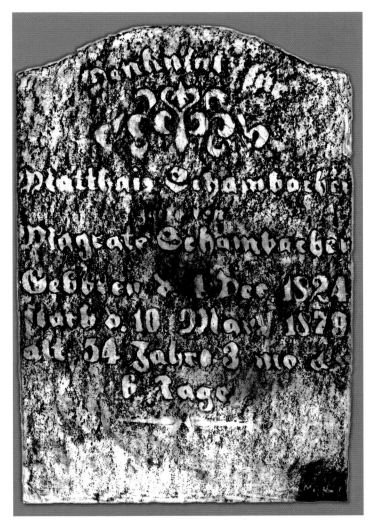

A RUBBING OF THE TOMBSTONE OF MATTHIAS SCHAMBACHER

MAURICE AND IRMA BROUN AT SCHAUMBOCH'S IN 1959

THE FRONT PORCH AT SCHAUMBOCH'S IN AUTUMN

AMERICAN KESTREL OVER HUNTERS' FIELD

CHAPTER 5

Autumn flights

> *"The birds scud past on half-furled wings, riding the updraft along the west face of the ridge. Mile after mile of autumn landscape slips by below as if the hawk were stationary and the world was doing the traveling, or as if the bird were carried along on an invisible conveyor belt."*
>
> —Roger Tory Peterson,
> **Birds Over America, *1948***

Something about a raptor stirs the human heart and grips the mind.

Perhaps it is the grace with which they soar above the fray.

Perhaps it is the fierceness and abandon with which they attack their quarry.

Or maybe it is their pure athleticism. They are all business, these birds of prey: sharp talons, hooked beaks, muscular bodies and the keenest of eyes. No wonder, then, that they are at the top of the food chain.

And there's no better place to see them in the wild, on the wing, than at Hawk Mountain in autumn.

Not only does the sanctuary have the vistas and the expert spotters, but it also seems to attract genial, hawk-eyed birders willing to share their knowledge.

Part of raptor-watching is the sheer exhilaration one gets from seeing a bird of prey as it glides past. But at the lookouts, a friendly competition is often afoot as well, to be the first to spot the next raptor and—even better—identify it correctly.

MALE JUVENILE COOPER'S HAWK

When the hawks are plentiful, it is easy to get caught up in the excitement and start calling out whenever you see a distant speck.

Here is some simple advice that goes beyond bringing a good pair of binoculars, food and water, sunscreen and a thick cushion on which to sit.

When you arrive at one of the lookouts, you have the right to remain silent for a couple of minutes until you get into the rhythms of the day and a sense of proportion. Through binoculars, judging the size of a raptor can be difficult, especially when you arrive.

Nothing can be as intimidating to a casual birder as viewing hawks from a promontory with a group of experienced raptor watchers. The first challenge is to see the birds as they are pointed out— and it takes another leap of ability to accurately identify that bird.

Perhaps the worst-case scenario is blurting out a totally wrong ID.

Consider this unfortunate soul. One early September day not long ago, only a pair of resident turkey vultures was aloft near South Lookout. Breaking the silence, an eager birder announced he had just seen a kestrel. A Hawk Mountain staffer asked where.

The birder pointed to his right, and the staffer said, in a non-judgmental tone, "All I see is that chimney swift."

Many of the people at South Lookout no doubt breathed a sigh of relief and thought, "There but for the grace of God go I."

Almost every birder, novice and expert, has blurted out that sort of mistake and wished they had kept their mouth shut, or— better—wished they had asked what kind of bird it was instead of venturing some gut-reaction guess.

The good news is that aside from momentary embarrassment, such gaffes are no big deal. Anybody who takes the time to go to a hawk watch to look at raptors is already a step ahead of the rest of the population.

Besides, even experts don't always agree on an identification. One veteran raptor watcher tells of the time that he was with Maurice Broun, sanctuary president Joseph Taylor and top birder Gordon Meade.

"A bird came down across the valley, and Maurice said it was a peregrine," he recalls. "Joe and I said it was a redtail with its wings folded, and Gordon said it was a redshoulder. We decided that since it was Maurice's mountain, we wouldn't argue about it. Who knows what it was."

If you are looking for a top-notch field guide to migrating raptors, you might try *Hawks in Flight* by Pete Dunne, David Sibley and Clay Sutton. On the following pages are images of Hawk Mountain's most frequent fliers, along with thumbnail descriptions and quotations on them by notable naturalists—past and present.

BROAD-WINGED HAWK CLOSE UP

BROAD-WINGED HAWK

"Far away ... I saw a pair of wheeling buzzards and, under them, in lesser circles, a broad-winged hawk. Here, at the feet of the tall, clean trees, ... I had something of a measure for the flight of the birds. The majesty and the mystery of the distant buoyant wings were singularly impressive."

—*Dallas Lore Sharp*, **The Lay of the Land** *(1908)*

Along with the golden eagle, the broad-winged hawk is Hawk Mountain's signature bird. Each autumn, nearly half of all raptors counted at North Lookout typically are broadwings. Broadwings are crow-sized and known for their kettling—using pockets of rising warm air to gain altitude as they travel in large flocks during migration. Peak time to see these small buteos is mid-September, after a cold front.

- TEN-YEAR AVERAGE FALL CENSUS AT HAWK MOUNTAIN (1998-2007): 7,850.
- TOP ONE-YEAR TOTAL AT HAWK MOUNTAIN: 29,519 (1978)
- EASTERN RANGE: New England and Canada to South America

ADULT BROAD-WINGED HAWK RISING ON A COLUMN OF AIR

JUVENILE BROAD-WINGED HAWK GLIDING

ADULT RED-SHOULDERED HAWK

RED-SHOULDERED HAWK

"Because of its secretive nature, the redshoulder is often first detected by its strident calls, which pierce the morning air from the Maine woods to the Corkscrew Swamp in Florida."

—*Clay Sutton and Patricia Taylor Sutton,*
How to Spot Hawks and Eagles *(1996)*

When nesting, these slightly larger relatives of broadwings are considered threatened in some states. They have long been associated with forests near water but are slowly adapting to suburbia in some areas. In flight, they flap and glide like accipiters, but they are seen far less often at Hawk Mountain than sharpies and Cooper's hawks. In flight, pale crescents can often be seen near the wing tips.

- TEN-YEAR AVERAGE: 270
- TOP ONE-YEAR TOTAL: 468 (1958)
- EASTERN RANGE: New England and Canada to Florida

Red-tailed Hawk

"Hawks are beautiful objects when on the wing. I have often stood to view a hawk in the sky trembling its wings and then hanging still for a moment as if it was as light as a shadow and could find like the clouds a resting place upon the still blue air."

—*John Clare*, Journal *(1820s)*

These even larger buteos are the raptors that perch along major highways and that prey on the squirrels in your back yard—one reason why they are the most commonly seen hawk in the United States. Hawk Mountain has had many resident redtails over the years. One sign of a redtail: It can hang motionless on the wind (a behavior called kiting).

- TEN-YEAR AVERAGE: 3,663
- TOP ONE-YEAR TOTAL: 6,208 (1939)
- RANGE: New England and Canada to Florida and Central America

RED-TAILED HAWK

OSPREY

OSPREY

"It skims over the lakes and rivers, and sometimes seems to lie extended on the water, as he hovers so close to it, and having by some attractive power draw the fish within its reach, darts suddenly upon him."

—*Anonymous,* Travels through the Interior Parts of North America *(1766)*

The osprey is a large, fish-eating raptor, hence the nickname "fish hawk." To see an osprey with a fish in its talons as it flies past Hawk Mountain is a feather in one's cap. One veteran observer claims to have seen three in a row just before lunch—his and theirs. Their population dwindled as a result of DDT and other pesticides but has made a strong comeback.

- TEN-YEAR AVERAGE: 631
- TOP ONE-YEAR TOTAL: 872 (1990)
- EASTERN RANGE: New England and Canada to Florida, the Caribbean, and South America

OSPREY WITH FISH

COOPER'S HAWK

"Possessing all the classic accipiter traits—short, rounded wings, a comparatively small head, and a long, darkly barred tail...this dashing bird of prey is truly a living, breathing work of art."

—*Floyd Scholz,* Birds of Prey *(1993)*

These crow-sized accipiters are less common than sharpies but almost as adept at navigating forests and nailing feeder birds. They are making a slow recovery after losing part of their population to DDT and other pesticides. At Hawk Mountain, sharpies and Coops can be seen migrating together, but at a ratio of roughly 13 to 1.

- TEN-YEAR AVERAGE: 834
- TOP ONE-YEAR TOTAL: 1,118 (1998)
- EASTERN RANGE: New England and Canada to Florida and Mexico

Sharp-shinned Hawk

"The flight of this hawk is so peculiar that it can be easily recognized in the distance. It is swift, vigorous, and somewhat varied and irregular."

—*Thomas G. Gentry,* Life Histories of the Birds of Eastern Pennsylvania *(1877)*

Juvenile Sharp-shinned Hawk

A "sharpie" or "little blue darter" is an accipiter that is slightly larger than a blue jay. Its short, rounded wings and long tail enable it to steer through the forest understory and zip around backyard bird feeders. If a hawk is terrorizing your feeder birds, the sharpie is your prime suspect. It is also the raptor most likely to attack the owl decoy at North Lookout.

- Ten-year average: 4,452
- Top one-year total: 10,612 (1977)
- Eastern range: New England and Canada to Florida and the Caribbean

Northern goshawk over North Lookout
(Painting by Fred Wetzel)

Northern Goshawk

"The adult [goshawk] is as striking and beautiful as it is powerful—a shadow cast in gray, with piercing red eyes that radiate malevolence."

—*Pete Dunne, David Sibley and Clay Sutton*,
Hawks in Flight *(1988)*

This large accipiter migrates along the Kittatinny Ridge from mid-October to early December when food sources to the north are thin. It can be extremely aggressive when protecting its nest, to the point of attacking humans who venture too close. According to legend, Attila the Hun had the image of a goshawk on his helmet.

- Ten-year average: 61
- Top one-year total: 347 (1972)
- Eastern range: New England and Canada to Maryland

MERLIN

MERLIN

"It is a bold and dashing little falcon and has no hesitation in attacking birds larger than itself...."
　　　　　—*Arthur Cleveland Bent,* Life Histories of North American Birds of Prey *(1937)*

This pigeon-sized falcon is another fast flier occasionally seen at Hawk Mountain. Like other falcons, it tends to migrate along the coast. Although it is typically a bird of the woodlands, it is being seen increasingly in urban areas.

- TEN-YEAR AVERAGE: 157
- TOP ONE-YEAR TOTAL: 231 (2007)
- EASTERN RANGE: Northeast and Canada to Florida and the Caribbean

AMERICAN KESTREL

AMERICAN KESTREL

"Beautifully erect, it stands on the highest fence-stake, the broken top of a tree, the summit of a grain stack, or the corner of the barn, patiently and silently waiting until it espies a mole, a field-mouse, a cricket, or a grasshopper, on which to pounce."

—*John James Audubon,* Birds of America *(1840)*

This colorful falcon has sometimes been called a sparrow hawk. It is the size of a dove and can be seen perching near farmland when it hunts. It is the most common—and smallest—falcon seen from North Lookout, although it has been in a decline in many parts of the Northeast. Kestrels migrate past Hawk Mountain in the biggest numbers in early October.

- TEN-YEAR AVERAGE: 527
- TOP ONE-YEAR TOTAL: 839 (1989)
- EASTERN RANGE: Northeast and Canada to Florida

PEREGRINE FALCON

PEREGRINE FALCON

"Like the seafarer, the peregrine lives in a pouring-away world of no attachment, a world of wakes and tilting, of sinking planes of land and water."

—*J.A. Baker,* Peregrine *(1967)*

The peregrine falcon, occasionally called a duck hawk, has made a remarkable rebound in the Northeast after DDT and other pesticides had eradicated that population. These birds are powerful, blazingly fast, and—since they are uncommon to begin with—a real treat to see on the wing. Peregrine means "wanderer." The range of these birds explains how they got their name.

- TEN-YEAR AVERAGE: 50
- TOP ONE-YEAR TOTAL: 62 (2006)
- RANGE: Northeast and Canada to Chile

GOLDEN EAGLE

GOLDEN EAGLE

"I have spent a great deal of time watching eagles, and have never ceased to be filled with childlike wonder at the great birds. 'The way of an eagle in the air' is a vision of inexpressible grace, arousing our deepest poetic instincts and filling us with pure delight."

—Maurice Broun, Hawks Aloft *(1949)*

The golden eagle, with its seven-foot span and its prevalence on many continents, is known as "the king of birds." At Hawk Mountain it is particularly revered. It was here that Maurice Broun determined that—contrary to prevailing belief—golden eagles occurred regularly in the American Northeast during migration. The Hawk Mountain insignia patch has a golden eagle on it.

- ▪ TEN-YEAR AVERAGE: 120
- ▪ TOP ONE-YEAR TOTAL: 164 (2006)
- ▪ EASTERN RANGE: New England and Canada to the southern Appalachians

BALD EAGLE

BALD EAGLE

"He sees the forests like a carpet beneath him; he sees the hills and valleys as folds and wrinkles in a many-colored tapestry; he sees the river as a silver belt connecting remote horizons. We climb mountain peaks to get a glimpse of the spectacle that is hourly spread out beneath him."

—John Burroughs, Far and Near *(1904)*

The bald eagle, the symbol of the United States, has an impressive seven-foot wingspan. The "bald" part of its name is short for "piebald," meaning "spotted or patched, especially with black and white." The adult bald eagle is hard to mistake. Its body and wings are deep brown and its head and tail are white. The bald eagle is making a strong recovery in the Northeast in the post-DDT era.

- TEN-YEAR AVERAGE: 201
- TOP ONE-YEAR TOTAL: 260 (2008)
- EASTERN RANGE: Northeast and Canada to Florida

FEMALE NORTHERN HARRIER

NORTHERN HARRIER

"The marsh hawk quarters its hunting territory, tacking first in one direction, then another, then back, a pattern that has given it its other name, 'harrier' (after the harehounds—harriers—that hunt rabbits in the same zigzagging way)."

—*Michael Harwood,* The View from Hawk Mountain *(1973)*

Harriers are typically seen hunting low over wetlands, wheeling back and forth often as they methodically scan the ground for prey. With feathered discs around their eyes, their faces appear owl-like. The male, white underneath with gray head, back and wings, is known as "the gray ghost." The female is various shades of brown. Both male and female have a white rump.

- ANNUAL AVERAGE: 240
- TOP ONE-YEAR TOTAL: 475 (1980)
- EASTERN RANGE: Northeast and Canada to Florida

ADULT MALE NORTHERN HARRIER

BLACK VULTURE

"With a heavier, more thickset body than the turkey buzzard and shorter wings, this very common 'carrion crow' may be identified in mid-air by its comparative lack of grace in flight, its frequent wing-flapping and its smaller size...."

—*Neltje Blanchan*, Birds that Hunt and are Hunted (*1898*)

Black vultures, once rarities in the Northeast, are now regular inhabitants. The first year that one was seen at Hawk Mountain was 1969. With flatter wings than their turkey-vulture cousins, they are more readily mistaken for other raptors. They are often seen in pairs—and sometimes called "buzzards" by non-birders.

- TEN-YEAR AVERAGE: 67
- TOP ONE-YEAR TOTAL: 140 (2007)
- EASTERN RANGE: New England and lower Canada to the South

TURKEY VULTURE

"The turkey vulture is ugly to the last degree, except in flight....
Its circling form, on motionless, widely outstretched pinions, is
seldom absent from the skyscape of its habitat as it soars in great
circles, scanning the ground below."

—*T. Gilbert Pearson*, Birds of America *(1936)*

Turkey vultures are eagle-sized raptors with red heads, dark-brownish bodies and a "V" or dihedral shape to their wings when gliding. They also have a tendency to wobble in flight, resembling a child riding a bicycle with training wheels. These birds have a sense of smell that enables them to detect dead animals from far above. Resident turkey vultures roost near Owl's Head and elsewhere in the sanctuary.

- TEN-YEAR AVERAGE: 338
- TOP ONE-YEAR TOTAL: 636 (2007)
- RANGE: Southern Canada to southern South America

TURKEY VULTURE

The cinnamon light of late autumn

CHAPTER 6

A sanctuary year

> "To the attentive eye, each movement of the year has its own beauty, and in the same field it beholds, every hour, a picture which was never seen before and which shall never be seen again…. The tribes of birds and insects, like the plants punctual to their time, follow each other, and the year has room for all."
>
> —Ralph Waldo Emerson, Nature, 1836

Hawk Mountain will always be a magnet for those who seek to observe migrating raptors. But it also is a sanctuary for humans, and a beguiling place year-round, often more for what is on the ground than for what is in the sky.

As the seasons ebb and flow, the Kittatinny Ridge is constantly changing. Yet, in all the ways that matter, it remains forever the same. Here is a sense of the sanctuary when hawk-watching season is not in full swing—from December through August.

DECEMBER

The leaves on the red maples, chestnut oaks and black gums have disappeared, long gone with the raptors and the crowds. The sanctuary winds down from another season of migration, and the amount of daylight dwindles. The sun and its warmth fade before afternoon's end.

Dusk offers an unusual tinge this time of year. As a few brave souls head down the rocky trail from North Lookout after a chilly, day-long vigil of raptor-counting, a reddish glow bathes the mountainside. One Hawk Mountain volunteer calls it "cinnamon light."

SOUTH LOOKOUT IN WINTER

JANUARY

On a hike to the North Lookout, a light coating of snow foretells a blizzard two weeks away. The trail is frozen under foot, with only footprints of a few other humans and a lone raccoon.

The woods seem quieter than usual. No wind buffets the skeletal tree branches, and the snow muffles other sounds. Little is heard but a chickadee—Maurice Broun's favorite bird—repeating its singsong, three-note call.

After the vigorous walk and climb to North Lookout, you feel nice and warm at first. But the mercury is stuck near 20 degrees and, even without a wind, the cold soon creeps through your boots and gloves.

The only sign of life is a gray squirrel, and it soon heads off in search of shelter. One thinks back to autumn, when the lookout was jammed with people. Now it is silent and stone still. The pit is now empty, save for clumps of snow.

The decoy of the great horned owl, high above the ground on its skinny wooden pedestal, looks a little more weather-beaten and bedraggled than usual. The mountain laurel looks defeated, curled and hanging limp on bushes that seemed so vibrant in autumn.

EDUCATIONAL SIGNS NEAR SOUTH LOOKOUT HELP VISITORS IDENTIFY RAPTORS AND EXPLAIN THE MIGRATION PHENOMENON.

To the west, the ponds are frozen, and the Little Schuylkill River is iced over. The sky is empty, without so much as a turkey vulture in sight. The views are still splendid.

To stand in solitude, with the sweeping vistas of the mountains and valleys all to yourself, is to be the richest person in the world.

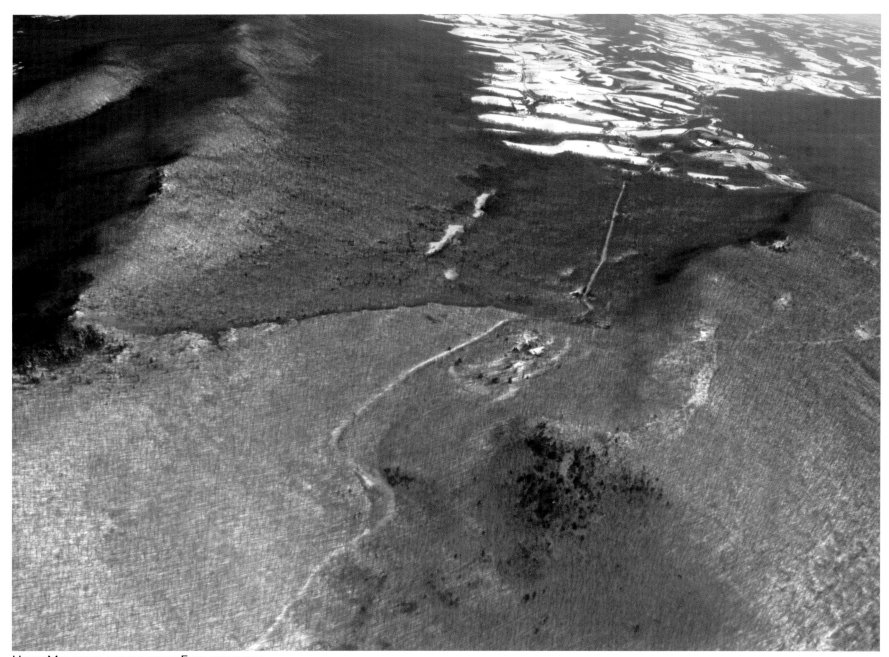

Hawk Mountain after a heavy February snow

Hawk Mountain in winter
A bird's-eye view

To fly over a snow-covered Hawk Mountain is to experience sensory overload.

For the aerial photograph on the facing page, photographer Kevin Watson and I chartered a Cessna out of Lehigh Valley International Airport. The blizzard of February 2007 had ripped through the region a couple of days earlier, and nearby Interstate 78 was still closed. The only way to get to Hawk Mountain, it turned out, was by plane.

By the time our plane reached 3,400 feet, we felt raptor-like as we surveyed the terrain below.

From ground level, the mountain seems steep, especially that final stretch to North Lookout. From the sky, the mountain resembled a large wrinkle in the patchwork of forest and farms.

On this winter's day, the landscape was strikingly atonal, mostly white and dark brown, with an occasional deep green of a pine. The mountain's surface, covered with snow and skeletal trees, had the look of a wolf's fur.

As we approached the ridge, we became sightseers, spotting landmarks that cried out for recognition: the River of Rocks, North Lookout, the Visitor Center.

To fly over Hawk Mountain engenders a sense of freedom, a sense of exhilaration—especially on a day when the snow still played havoc with stranded motorists and other earth-bound creatures.

Then, as we crossed the ridge by North Lookout, we were buffeted by a 30-mile-an-hour gust—the sort of updraft that the hawks take for granted and use to glide southward.

From on high, we also gained an appreciation for raptors' phenomenal eyesight. The best digital camera with a super-size telephoto lens cannot begin to capture distant images with the clarity of a raptor's eyes. By one estimate, a redtail can spot a mouse a mile away.

Our bird's-eye view was vast. The Cessna's pilot estimated that our visibility was roughly 30 miles: "Endless Mountain" indeed.

With that vista came a newfound admiration for the raptors that fly past the sanctuary every autumn. In a day they can travel up to 300 miles—ten times as far as our human eyes could see from the air on that February day.

—Jim Wright

COUNTER'S PIT AT NORTH LOOKOUT IN WINTER

FEBRUARY

In the predawn chill, the walk to South Lookout is quiet and quick. To the southeast, a gash of light cuts through the thick gray clouds on the horizon, and another day begins.

As that gash grows more intense, going from crimson to hot-ember orange, the valley slowly embraces the light, and dawn becomes day.

Aside from the sound of a solitary car driving over the mountain, the world of the sanctuary is tranquil in the dawn's early light. It is a time to be lost in thought, unless the thought includes how cold your fingers and toes are getting.

Nonetheless, as you watch the dawn, you cannot help but think that far to the east, your sunrise is another person's sunset. The world continues to spin, clocking days the way an odometer logs miles.

To watch the dawn from Hawk Mountain in February offers fresh perspectives. For those who have made the trek many times before and have accumulated a scrapbook's worth of sunrises and sunsets, of crisp autumn days and an endless flow of raptors overhead, the view from South Lookout is filled with warm memories on a cold morning.

PUSSYWILLOW

MARCH

The trail to the North Lookout is mostly clear, with a few pockets of melting snow. You encounter just one hiker on the trail. Instead of binoculars, he carries a mug of coffee.

At North Lookout, two turkey vultures laze overhead. Soon, a skein of northbound Canada geese appears in an undulating line, and although they may not be migrating raptors, it seems good to see them after so little airborne activity in prior months.

The valleys are beginning their annual renewal. The distant ponds have thawed. The landscape starts to turn green again. Like the swallows of Capistrano, the phoebes of Hawk Mountain return to nest under the eaves of the trail entryway.

A couple and their children are at North Lookout for the first time in six years. They say they love where they live in western Pennsylvania—they just came here to experience someone else's bit of heaven.

They notice the changes in the landscape since their last visit—the wind turbines on the western horizon, a few more large homes in the valley.

They also note that the rocks of North Lookout have not changed at all, and they find it reassuring.

BLOODROOT IN APRIL

APRIL

The temperature is in the low 40s, with a light breeze. There's a mist in the valley to the right of Donat, and on the River of Rocks trail, trees are just starting to bud again.

The trail in spring is a trail of sounds as much as sights. In the breeze float the calls of a hermit thrush and a downy woodpecker, and the baleful hoo…hoo…hoo of a lone mourning dove.

Along the trail, the trunks of decaying pines bear the rectangular holes of pileated woodpeckers. A cascade of kinglets ripples past, followed by a tail-twitching palm warbler.

The sun burns hot in the deep blue sky as you navigate the River of Rocks trail, and you eventually realize that although you never cross that river of stones, the trail is aptly named. Even if you are nimble of foot and wielding a walking stick, you do not hike so much as navigate the impossibly rocky terrain.

No wonder that hikers call the nearby stretch of the Appalachian Trail "the place where boots go to die."

RHODODENDRON IN BLOOM AT SOUTH LOOKOUT

PINK LADY'S SLIPPER

THE INDIGO BUNTING AT SOUTH LOOKOUT

MAY

This may be the month when you can best appreciate the mountain for its landscape. The hemlocks and other trees show new growth, and the dogwoods along Hawk Mountain Road are in bloom.

By mid-month, the chlorophyll in the new leaves is at its most vibrant green, and the air is warm enough for visitors to plunk themselves down at a rock outcropping without catching cold.

Jack-in-the-pulpits are sprouting, the trillium and other flowers are blossoming. Not too far off the path by the Visitor Center, a pink lady's slipper blooms.

The main attraction at South Lookout is a male indigo bunting that apparently has a nesting female nearby. He seems to have a circuit of perches, and one of them is on a hemlock by South Lookout. Every so often, he appears in his stunning blue wardrobe and performs his favorite song.

On a warbler walk by Pine Swamp Road, few songbirds are seen but many are heard—including blue-wingeds, common yellowthroats, hoodeds and yellows. A woman on the walk says she loves to travel and has been to all 50 states, but she calls Hawk Mountain home and loves it best of all.

JUNE

Each visit to Hawk Mountain's Native Plant Garden brings new sights and insights. On this day the air is warm before 10 a.m., and the dragonflies and butterflies are already out. A green darner darts about the lily pads and the waterlilies have bloomed to welcome the arrival of summer.

The swamp roses are out as well, and a green frog lazily calls from across the pond. A green darner suns itself on a twig by the observation area. Nearby, the newts swim just below the surface of the pond.

Several fritillaries cluster at the dogbane. The swamp roses attract bumblebees.

At South Lookout, a family of wild turkeys appears for a few days. The mountain laurel is peaking. The indigo bunting sings from a branch above the lookout. A scarlet tanager is a flash of red as it darts toward the trees nearby.

On the walk to North Lookout, the woods are alive with the calls of birds, the rustle of chipmunks and the buzz of insects. The hike feels different, with the path narrower because of the growth of all the greenery.

July

At South Lookout, early in the month and late in the evening, a full moon rises, partly obscured by clouds.

From the west, through the darkness, comes the rumble of a freight train. To the east, a distant fireworks display lights up a corner of the sky.

Later, the high-pitched squeaks of a little brown bat interrupt a sky that is empty save for the murmur of breeze through the

BUMBLEBEE AT THE RHODODENDRON

trees. More and more lights in the valley beyond South Lookout go dark, and evening turns into night.

Come morning, on the road from Kempton to the sanctuary, mist rises from the ponds as the full moon sets over Pinnacle. Ahead, a family of white-tailed deer crosses the road just below Schaumboch's.

On the porch of the old house, the marigolds and other flowers provide a burst of color that outshines and outlasts the fireworks of the night before. *(Text continues on page 106.)*

Nifty insects and amphibians abound in the Native Plant
Garden pond throughout the warm seasons.

BUMBLEBEE ON PICKEREL WEED IN THE NATIVE PLANT GARDEN

RABBIT ALONG THE PATH IN THE NATIVE PLANT GARDEN

SOLOMON'S SEAL IN THE NATIVE PLANT GARDEN

EASTERN PHOEBE PERCHED ON A SANCTUARY TALLY BOARD

AUGUST

In the fields in the mountain's shadow, corn is king and ready for harvest.

Swallowtails dot the roadsides and gardens, working the miniature bouquets of lavender joe-pye weed and almost every flower's bloom they see. In stark contrast to the gentle butterflies' beauty, webworms' tents mar tree branches along the region's roads.

At North Lookout, a few leaves have begun to turn burgundy. Already, chimney swifts are zipping past the lookout on the way south, and there have been reports of a bald eagle and several smaller raptors jumping the gun on the August 15 start of the autumn hawk count.

The daylight hours grow shorter, and the heat of the day disappears with the sun. The endless clouds, taken for granted most of the year, will soon once again provide the backdrop for nature's greatest air show.

Night brings the Perseid meteor shower. For hawk watchers, they are nature's annual reminder that the time has come to look to the skies once again.

FOXTAILS IN THE KEMPTON VALLEY

Pileated woodpecker near the Appalachian Trail next to Hawk Mountain

Eastern tiger swallow-tail on chokeberry in the Native Plant Garden

King corn in August, with Hawk Mountain in background

Hawk Mountain's Acopian Center at dusk

CHAPTER 7

The future

> *"The time to protect a species is while it is still common. The way to prevent the extinction of a species is never to let it become rare."*
>
> —Rosalie Edge,
> Emergency Conservation Committee
> report, 1933

To the occasional autumn visitor to Hawk Mountain, Keith Bildstein is the well-spoken, informative naturalist you see perched on a prominent rock at South Lookout. When his binoculars aren't trained on the sky, he's usually identifying distant raptors and fielding questions about hawks, migration and the sanctuary.

But most of the time Bildstein is the director of Hawk Mountain's Acopian Center for Conservation Science. One of the foremost raptor biologists in the world, he has studied migration on four continents.

What is the most important thing about Hawk Mountain?

A lot of people think of Hawk Mountain as a special place because of its birds, and it is special because of that. But it is unique because of the way that people and birds interact here.

There's no place on the surface of the earth that manages to show people birds of prey better than Hawk Mountain Sanctuary.

KEITH BILDSTEIN

How has raptor-migration science changed?

The most significant change is we now have the capacity to follow the long-distance migrations of individual raptors on a daily basis. You never had that before.

Banding a bird told us where it was banded and where it was recaptured or found dead. But that's a straight-line relationship, and nature doesn't usually travel in straight lines.

Satellite tracking now allows us to monitor the movements of individual birds across the surface of the planet.

Why is that important?

To me, that's something of a Holy Grail. To monitor the movements of individuals as opposed to the movements of populations allows us to probe the intimate biology of birds of prey. We weren't able to do that two decades ago.

Today, we are able to place the counts we've had here at Hawk Mountain over 75 years into an individual-bird perspective. We're going to take the satellite-tracked movements of ospreys and layer them using our geographical information system onto a map of the location of individual migration watch sites and be able to estimate the percentage of ospreys that are actually being counted. That gives us a better idea of the representative nature of those migration counts.

Maurice Broun, in his wildest dreams, wouldn't have been able to think about doing that. This emerging technology is going to take us farther faster than anything before.

Could you give an example?

We've been working with the Falcon Research Group in Washington State to place satellite telemetry units on male peregrines. Until recently you could not put a unit on males because there wasn't a unit small enough not to interfere with the behavior of the smaller male.

Two units were placed on male peregrines in northern Chile,

and one of them ended up in northwesternmost Arctic Canada. The other one over-summered in southernmost Baffin Island near Greenland. On its outbound journey in autumn, the latter shot down eastern Canada, eastern New York State and the Kittatinny Ridge, as far as Hawk Mountain. It actually roosted for a night about 400 meters from the Visitor Center, and then took off for the coast.

That's how precise satellite tracking is.

What are the biggest threats to raptors?

The three big threats to raptors are habitat loss, direct persecution, and environmental contamination. Of the three, the one we know the least about is environmental contaminants. The state of our ignorance is enormous.

I will give you an example. We lost two of the most common species of large raptors in the world over the last 20 years because of the widespread use of the veterinary drug Diclofenac. It's the equivalent of aspirin, a painkiller for cows.

The Asian white-backed vulture and the long-billed vulture were the common vultures on the Indian subcontinent. At doses that are appropriate for cows, Diclofenac is highly toxic to vultures that eat cows that die with this drug in their system. Diclofenac has now been banned in both Pakistan and India.

A PEREGRINE FALCON WITH A SMALL SATELLITE TELEMETRY UNIT

What's the answer?

To replace it with a nontoxic anti-inflammatory drug. One exists, and that has been proposed as a substitute. The tradeoff is that it's more expensive.

What's the big deal about losing these two species of vultures?

Scavengers play an important role in all ecosystems. Avian scavengers are especially important in removing dead animals, which are wonderful places for all kinds of potentially dangerous bacteria to occur. Nature abhors a vacuum, and the vultures' replacement in India has been small wild and feral dogs, and the occurrence of rabies has skyrocketed. There's a direct human consequence to the loss of these birds.

In retrospect, I don't think there's any conservationist who would have said that if you use this drug, you will have problems.

What about the shooting of raptors?

Shooting hawks is not a problem in Pennsylvania anymore. That doesn't mean it doesn't happen. Even so, the notion that there are good hawks and bad hawks is one of those things that exists in all societies and can come up at any time.

It's really important we recognize that this whole idea of controlling raptor populations, whether through shooting or other ways, is— I would argue—universally unsound.

What about climate change?

I think what we're beginning to see in terms of raptor migration suggests climate change may have a greater effect on migration than anyone has anticipated.

So far, all the arguments about climate change have been about how it is going to affect individual populations, the timing of migrations, and so forth. What we're starting to see is signals that global warming is reducing the likelihood of migration itself.

A world without migration is a world without migratory birds. What would that mean?

We could still have red-tailed hawks or peregrine falcons, but they wouldn't be migrating, or they'd migrate in smaller numbers. Everyone says, what's the difference? My argument is that raptor migration is an exceptional phenomenon that in and of itself is biologically significant.

There's a bird called the Hawaiian hawk, and it got to Hawaii because of raptor migration—not because there were raptors in North America but because there were migratory raptors in North America. The closest living relative of the Hawaiian hawk is also the closest relative of the Galapagos hawk, and that's the Swainson's hawk.

If Swainson's hawks stop migrating from North America to South America but still exist in North America, two things would happen. They will exist only on one continent, so their biological

WIND TURBINES NOW LOOM ON THE DISTANT HORIZON FROM NORTH LOOKOUT.

significance in South America will have disappeared. And they will no longer be a species that might give rise to a variety of island forms.

It's not just the players, it's what the players do that determines how ecosystems function. It's the migration itself that sends millions of birds every year thousands of miles. Most of them wind up where they're supposed to be. Others die en route.

And others still get pushed to different places and speciate [evolve into new species]. The Hawaiian hawk is a perfect example. The Galapagos hawk is a perfect example. You lose migration and you lose an important "engine" of biological diversity.

What is the biggest threat to Hawk Mountain?

The biggest threat would be that people stopped caring about raptors.

Why would that happen?

Because many in the federal government have already stopped caring. They stopped caring when the birds went from being endangered to not endangered, when they went from being uncommon to common.

Rosalie Edge founded Hawk Mountain on a principle, and the principle was: The time to conserve a species is while it is still common. Now many hawks are common. If we lose sight of Mrs. Edge's principle and all of a sudden decide to do something else, that would be a mistake.

But that is not going to happen at Hawk Mountain.

A view of The Kettle from North Lookout in autumn, when the raptors and foliage reign.

SUNRISE FROM SOUTH LOOKOUT

Index

Pages showing photographs or art are in italic.

RAPTOR-WATCHING AT NORTH LOOKOUT

A RED-TAILED HAWK GLIDES PAST NORTH LOOKOUT.

Acknowledgments

We must begin by thanking the incredibly capable folks at Hawk Mountain Sanctuary, including Lee Schisler Jr., Keith Bildstein, Mary Linkevich, Laurie Goodrich, David Barber, Sue Wolfe, Todd Bauman and Tirah Keal.

Jeremy Scheivert, Bob Owens, and the other staff, interns and volunteers at Hawk Mountain also could not have been more knowledgeable, congenial and helpful.

We wish to thank Fred Wetzel not only for his two paintings, but also for sharing his raptor know-how and his memories of the sanctuary in earlier times.

Over the course of our research, we interviewed dozens of people with long or strong ties to Hawk Mountain. These include Jim Brett, Deborah Edge, Mary Bailey, George Hamm, Charlie Gant, Warner Berthoff, Scott Weidensaul, Seth Benz, Minturn Wright, Stephen Oresman, Arlene Koch, Rudy Keller, David Hughes, Cliff Jones, Polly Hartnett, Kenneth Grimm, Jean Litzenberger, Bob Lynn, Robin Fitch, Eugene Rohrbach, Sue Schweitzer, George Miller, Sue Schmoyer and others. We thank them for all their help and patience.

We wish to thank Daniel Klem Jr. and Peter Saenger of Muhlenberg College for access to the Maurice Broun archives there.

We wish to thank Stiles and Lillian Thomas for all their help, support and inspiration. More than 50 years ago, Stiles founded the Mount Peter Hawk Watch in New York State, where J.W. first developed his interest in raptors.

We wish to thank Reed Andariese of AVICS, Inc. in Wyckoff, New Jersey, for his expertise, guidance and assistance in the preparation of the images for this book.

We wish to thank R.H. Kane for his help in creating the panoramic photo on pages 52 and 53.

Any errors in this book are the fault and responsibility of the authors.

A last word

Every September, about the time the broadwings are kettling, a group of longtime Hawk Mountaineers gathers at South Lookout to trade stories, catch up on news and continue unofficial traditions.

One is sharing a chocolate treat called Wilbur Buds, made for more than a century in Lititz, a town 50 miles to the southwest.

The other is enjoying a slice of Mountain Cake, a delicacy that has been served on paper plates at the two main lookouts since the 1970s.

It all began when Jean Litzenberger, a longtime volunteer, brought up some homemade molasses cake on several occasions during broadwing time. A woman from Ohio was so smitten by the concoction she proclaimed: "We have to give this the name of Mountain Cake."

The cake has gone by that name ever since, and it serves as a reminder that Hawk Mountain is not only about raptors and ridges, but the people and traditions that help make this remarkable place more than the sum of its parts.

PACK BASKETS AND MOUNTAIN CAKE ARE HAWK MOUNTAIN TRADITIONS.

MOUNTAIN CAKE

- Mix together 4 cups of flour, 2 cups of sugar and ½ pound of butter at room temperature (do not substitute).

- Take out about ¾ of a cup of the mixture for the topping.

- Add 2 cups of boiling water, 1 cup of Brer Rabbit molasses and 1 tablespoon of baking soda.

- Alternate the water with the molasses while mixing.

- Grease and flour a 9-by-13-inch pan. Pour mixture into pan and add the topping. Bake 40 to 45 minutes at 350 degrees.

Best served in mid-September at Hawk Mountain

Of Related Interest. . .

In the Presence of Nature

The Celery Farm Natural Area
Allendale, New Jersey

Photography by Jerry Barrack • Text by Jim Wright

"Spectacular pictures...show the diversity of plant and animal life that still exists [there]."
—The New York Times

Just miles from New York City, more than 100 acres of preserved open space known as the Celery Farm Natural Area provide a refuge for an astounding variety of wildlife—from herons, ducks, minks and foxes to many dozens of species of flowers and other protected plants. This beautiful book presents matchless color photographs of the inhabitants in every season of the year. The accompanying text details the history of the Celery Farm and the efforts of those who fought to save it.

128 pages
140 photographs
8.5 by 11 inches
Hardcover
$35.00

www.caminobooks.com